Technically, It's Not My Fault

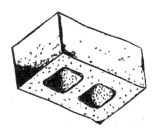

These poems were written on a Macintosh G4 using QuarkXPress Software.
The drawings were done with a Bristol China Marker and touched up in Adobe Photoshop.
The poems are set in the following typefaces:

Airstream ITC
Angryhog ITC
Bembo
Caflisch Script
Centaur
CHARLEMAGNE
Clover ITC
Courier New
Django ITC
Fenice ITC
Galliard ITC
Adobe Garamond
Gill Sans Condensed
Goudy Old Style
Grapefruit ITC
Jiggery Pokery ITC
Jott
Kristen Normal ITC
Kumquat ITC
Lingo ITC
Lubalin Graph
Lucida Handwriting
Ludwig ITC
Marker Felt
Medici Script
Sand
Stone Informal
Stone Sans
Tapioca ITC
TRAJAN
Uncle Stinky
&
✳❀□❊ ❖❊■✳❂❀▼▲ (Zapf Dingbats)

Technically, It's Not My Fault

Concrete Poems by John Grandits

Clarion Books   New York

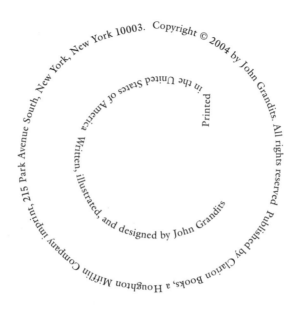
www.houghtonmifflinbooks.com

Printed in the U.S.A.

Library of Congress Cataloging-in-Publication Data
Grandits, John.
Technically, it's not my fault : concrete poems / by John Grandits
p. cm.
CL ISBN 0-618-42833-X
PA ISBN 0-618-50361-7
1. Concrete poetry, American. 2. Children's poetry, American. I Title
PS3607.R363B73 2004
811'.6—dc22   2004000231

CL ISBN-13: 978-0-618-42833-5
CL ISBN-10: 0-618-42833-X

PA ISBN-13: 978-0-618-50361-2
PA ISBN-10: 0-618-50361-7

WCP   10 9 8 7 6 5 4 3 2

Thanks to Mom and James and Andrea and Marcia and Dinah and Ramey Matt and Bagel Joe and Elm Place Lillian and Stellar Linda and Skateboard Communist.

For
Joanne & Jordan

These poems were written on a Macintosh G4 using QuarkXPress Software.
The drawings were done with a Bristol China Marker and touched up in Adobe Photoshop.
The poems are set in the following typefaces:

Airstream ITC
Angryhog ITC
Bembo
Caflisch Script
Centaur
CHARLEMAGNE
Clover ITC
Courier New
Django ITC
Fenice ITC
Galliard ITC
Adobe Garamond
Gill Sans Condensed
Goudy Old Style
Grapefruit ITC
Jiggery Pokery ITC
Jott
Kristen Normal ITC
Kumquat ITC
Lingo ITC
Lubalin Graph
Lucida Handwriting
Ludwig ITC
Marker Felt
Medici Script
Sand
Stone Informal
Stone Sans
Tapioca ITC
TRAJAN
Uncle Stinky
&
✳❂□❄ ❦❄■✳❂❀▼▲ (Zapf Dingbats)

MY STUPID DAY

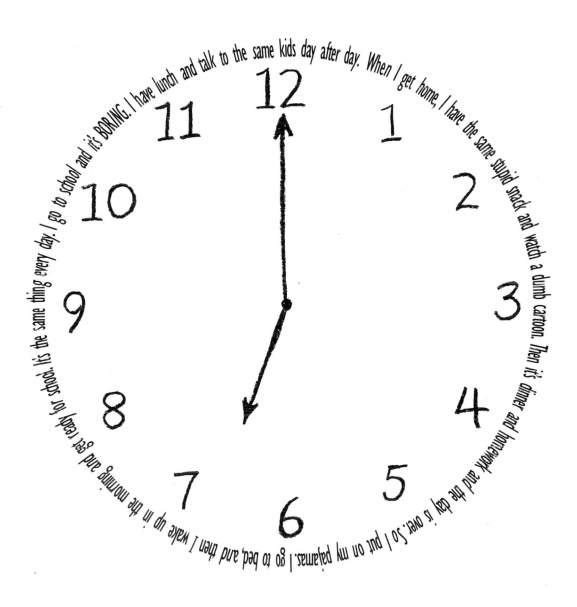

MY SISTER IS CRAZY

My sister wears a
pyramid on her head.
That's right. She has a
little pyramid-shaped hat.
"What is wrong with you?"
I ask her. "You look like a jerk!"
My sister sighs and rolls her eyes,
as if I'm the one who's a total loon.

"The pyramid is a source of ancient power,"
she says. "The Egyptians had pyramids, and
their empire lasted 3,000 years. The Aztecs ruled
Mexico with an iron fist. Or was it the Incas? No, Aztecs,
I think. Anyway, they had pyramids. And how about the
pyramid on the one-dollar bill? Coincidence? I don't think so."

My sister is crazy. That's because she's getting bombarded by alien
anti-brain waves from outer space. Super-intelligent beings from the
Nebula Galaxy are shooting at us with pluton rays that can make you
go crazy. They're not aiming at everyone, of course. Just my family.

That's why I wear aluminum foil on my head. I have a very good looking
ray-deflecting foil hat that I made myself. Not in the shape of a pyramid!
You'd have to be nuts to think that a pyramid would protect your brain from
evil alien rays coming from outer space. Which proves my point: My sister is crazy.

The Thank-You Letter[1]

Dear Aunt Hildegard,

Thank you[2] for the amazing gifts.[3] It was terrific[4] getting your package![5] I grabbed it immediately.[6] But when my parents saw it,[7] they said[8] I shouldn't open it until my birthday. You can imagine how I felt when I found two gifts![9] The sweater was totally awesome.[10] It's amazing how well you know me.[11]

Then there was the poster you got for my room.[12] You're in luck; I don't already have a Polka Hall of Fame poster.[13] I'm putting it right under my World Wrestling Federation poster.[14]

Thanks,[15] thanks,[16] and thanks again.[17] I'm already planning when to wear my new sweater.[18]

Your 11-year-old[19] nephew,

Robert

1. with Footnotes

2. For nothing!

3. Do you have the slightest clue what an 11-year-old boy likes?

4. I almost croaked when I saw the package. I still remember last year's gift. "Oh, no! Not again!" I screamed.

5. I was in luck. Mom didn't see the mailman.

6. I hid the package in the garage under the hose.

7. What were the chances that Dad would decide to wash the car *that* day?

8. "What's this?" they said. "When did this come?"

9. You monster.

10. In the history of sweaters, there has never been an uglier waste of yarn.

11. Where did you *ever* find a sweater that not only has Barney on it but also is two sizes too big for me?

12. I'm old enough to decorate my own room.

13. Just what I need—a picture of an old guy with an accordion.

14. And I do mean UNDER.

15. For trying to embarrass me in front of my friends.

16. For the lectures from my parents.

17. For making me waste an hour of my life writing this stupid thank-you letter.

18. I know they'll make me wear it the next time you come to visit. I just hope nobody sees me.

19. I'm 11!!! Get it?!?

TyrannosaurBus Rex

I am the vicious TyrannosaurBus Rex.
I roam the suburbs, hunting.
Those who see me gaze in terror.
Those who are spared are grateful.

Early in the morning, I spy
a group of small human children
standing on the corner of Elm and Spring.
I slam on my brakes.
I open my mouth.
"Come in, little children," I say.
They don't want to, but they must.
Their parents have delivered them to me.
Human sacrifices.

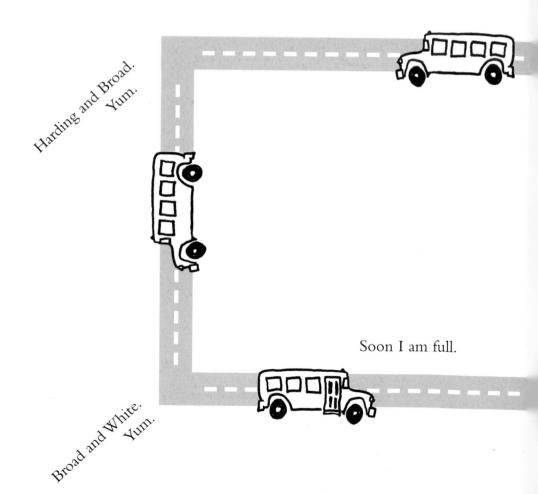

Harding and Broad.
Yum.

Soon I am full.

Broad and White.
Yum.

I eat the humans.
They are young and tender.
Yum.

Then I go to Elm and Hudson.
More children. More sacrifices.
Yum.

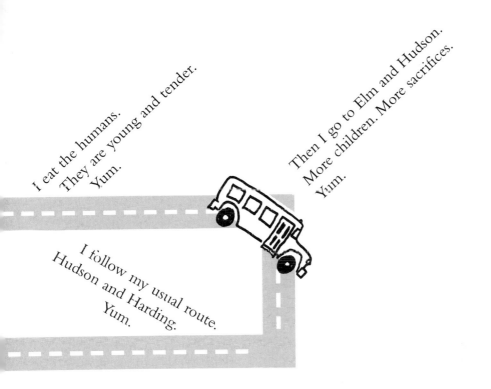

I follow my usual route.
Hudson and Harding.
Yum.

My breakfast is noisy.
My breakfast is jumping around
in my
stomach.
My breakfast is giggling and laughing and arguing.
My stomach is queasy.

I don't feel so good.

I go to the
school parking lot.
I open my mouth
and barf out my noisy,
jumping,
giggling,
laughing,
arguing
breakfast.

I'm so tired from hunting. I settle into my nap
and dream dreams about 3:30,
when I will go to the parking lot
next to the school and hunt again.

The Australian Cane Toad

The cane toad does not belong in Australia.
He doesn't like it much.
"How did I get here?" he asks himself.
"These Australian bugs taste awful."
Unfortunately for the toad, a dingo sneaks up from behind.
Snap! Crunch! Gulp! . . . Ahhh.
Unfortunately for the dingo, the cane toad is poisonous.
Very poisonous.

Cane Toad
Bufo marinus

Cane toads are not native to Australia. They were introduced in 1935 by sugar cane farmers in the hopes that they would eat the gray-back cane beetle and French's cane

beetle, pests that were destroying the sugar cane crop. Unfortunately, the toads have proved to be even bigger pests than the beetles. They eat large numbers of honeybees, prey on native fauna, and carry diseases that are transmitted to native frogs and fishes. They are also highly toxic.

If eaten or handled, cane toads can poison household pets and injure humans. They can also kill native species, including the goanna, tiger snake, northern spotted quoll, red-

bellied black snake, death adder, freshwater crocodile, and dingo.

Dingo
Canis lupus dingo

Dingoes are light gray or reddish tan doglike mammals that live throughout Australia in habitats ranging from harsh deserts to lush rainforests. They may have been brought to the continent 3,000 to 4,000 years ago as domestic animals, but at some point they became feral.

Dingoes are not pack animals like wolves. They hunt alone or in pairs, mostly at night. They prefer to eat small mammals such as rodents and rabbits, but they will also hunt large creatures such as kangaroo and sheep. When food is scarce, they will eat reptiles, amphibians, and insects.

I'm supposed to be doing my science homework.
But really I'm reading about the cane toad.
The homework sheet is about magnets.
It's stupid. Not only stupid, but easy.
We had all this stuff last year.
The teacher must think we're morons.
Well, some of us *are* morons,
so she's partially right.
It's just that *I'm* not a moron.
Multiple choice:

- ❑ One answer is right.
- ❑ Two are close if you're not paying attention.
- ❑ One is wrong.
- ❑ And one is you-must-not-have-the-brains-God-gave-a-chicken wrong.

I answer each question with the chicken-brain option.

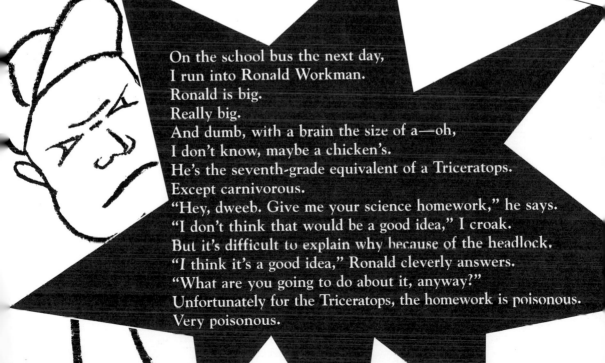

On the school bus the next day,
I run into Ronald Workman.
Ronald is big.
Really big.
And dumb, with a brain the size of a—oh,
I don't know, maybe a chicken's.
He's the seventh-grade equivalent of a Triceratops.
Except carnivorous.
"Hey, dweeb. Give me your science homework," he says.
"I don't think that would be a good idea," I croak.
But it's difficult to explain why because of the headlock.
"I think it's a good idea," Ronald cleverly answers.
"What are you going to do about it, anyway?"
Unfortunately for the Triceratops, the homework is poisonous.
Very poisonous.

SKATEBOARD

I'm on my totally cool new board and I'm bombing the hill. I do a little cut jump up a curb into the

lift onto the bench,

Out of the lot, curb, across the street, curb, into the park. I do a sweet little

Busted. Walking home. I'm a sad old dog who's been swatted with a rolled-up newspaper.

7-Eleven parking lot and try a tight little figure eight just to see how she corners, and I'm about to try a tricky little ollie over a milk crate when all of a sudden I hear HEY, KID! No skateboards in the parking lot. Get outta here!

land clean, p-u-u-u-m-p up the hill, around the flagpole, d-o-o-o-w-n the ramp, and HEY, YOU! Can't you read the sign? No skateboarding!

I give up. I'm just gonna veg in front of the TV and not think about it. I mean, why bother, and then HEY, What are you doing inside? You begged for that skateboard, Robert. Now go out and use it!

DRAWKCAB

Mrs. Kosacowski started it.
Last week in social studies class she said to me,
"Robert, sometimes I think you're brilliant,
and other times I think you're absolutely backward,
and that you act backward on purpose."

So I'm teaching myself
to be backward on purpose.

Today Mrs. K. asked,
"Robert, are you paying attention?"
"On, ton yllaer," I answered.
"What did you say?" she said.
"I ma gniklat drawkcab yadot," I explained.
"Oh, my goodness. Are you having a seizure?"
Mrs. K. looked a little worried.
"On, I ma enif." I tried to reassure her. "Tub ouy
thgim eb gninrael-deriapmi."
She sent me to the nurse's office.

"I ma yllaer yako," I told the nurse.
She called my mom anyway.
Mom will have to take off from work
to come pick me up.
But I'm not worried.
I can explain everything.
I just hope Mom understands drawkcab klat.

What Are You Thinking About, Robert?

Ronald Workman was showing off a pack of cigarettes in the boys' bathroom. What an idiot. Hope he gets caught.

Dickie Erickson says, "Marcia Feddleston likes you." So I say, "So what?" I'm a good person. Why shouldn't she like me?" And he goes, "Not that kind of likes you. I mean planning-the-honeymoon likes you."

WWE Smackdown is on at 11:00 tonight, but I'm supposed to be in bed at 10:30.

Why don't they make scratch-and-sniff fart stickers?

Another unit on Sacajawea?! Can't they find a different girl hero to bore us with?

My gym clothes weren't THAT bad. It's only been six weeks. You could still tell what color they were.

Marcia Feddleston came over to talk to me in the hall.

Got up late. No time for breakfast. Forgot my lunch. Only had 45 cents. Man, am I hungry.

I don't care HOW hungry I am. I hate cucumbers, and I'm not eating them.

Nothin'.

So when I was talking to my class today, I told them that they really had to have more respect for their teachers. Respect for the authority figure is what western civilization is built on. But I tried to put it to them in their own language. "Don't get *snarpy* with The Man," I said.
Oh, Bill, you are so hip! The kids must LOVE you.
What the heck is he talking about now?
My boyfriend, Bill, teaches seventh grade and he can't seem to leave his work at school. He's so-o-o-o juvenile. I think I've got to dump him. He's too *snarpy*.
So he's a little *snarpy*! So what! Don't be so picky.
Today on the Style Network: What's in? What's out? How do we know what the beautiful people are saying? Who decides what's hip? We go to our trend correspondent, Marsala Piquet. Marsala?
Thanks, Morton. In the past, when an older man—like yourself—said or did something new, it became fashion. Nowadays younger and younger kids are deciding what's hip and what's not, what's in and what's out. Fashion is made in middle school or even grammar school. Clothes, language, hair color, even what we eat and drink are determined by kids. But don't worry, Morton, we still think you're very *snarpy*! Back to you.
The president announced today that the country of Bizaristan faces strict censure and loss of trading privileges with the U.S. if it doesn't alter its foreign policy. CNN has this exclusive interview. . . . Mr. President, could you tell the American people -- what *is* the problem in Bizaristan?
In a nutshell, Wolf, it's their attitude. In the White House, we think they're a 10 on the *Snarpy*-Attitude Scale. If we don't address these issues now, the American people will suffer in the long run. That's why I am sending the secretary of state . . .
Wow! I guess *snarpy* really is a word.

THE TOWER

Rapunzel, Rapunzel, let down your hair, I said. And she did. I started climbing. Watch out for my hair, she said, I don't want split ends. Take your boots off, I just washed it, she said. Watch out for my barrette, it's my favorite! she said. Why are you slowing down? Aren't you strong enough to rescue me? Why did you stop? What kind of prince are you, anyway? I climbed back down. I've heard about this other princess who's asleep—a real beauty.

hair hair hair hair hair hair hair hair hair hair hair hair hair hair hair hair hair hair

How We Ended Up with a Plain Pizza

All right, all right!

Definitely NO green peppers. And NO onions. And NO garlic. And NO mushrooms. Mushrooms are just poisonous fungi that are dug out of the ground by pigs.

We'll order pizza. We have a coupon for one extra-large pie. But everybody has to agree on what toppings to get.

I don't care what you kids get on the pizza as long as there are anchovies on it.

Pizza's not pizza unless it's covered with sausage and pepperoni. Forget the slimy vegetables!

I refuse to eat anything with dead animals all over it. Do you know how those poor animals suffer just so you can fill your body with toxic grease?

I just don't think this family is eating properly. If we must have pizza, at least let's get some healthy toppings on it.

There's this pizza place downtown that has pineapple guava. I don't know what I think but I think we should try it.

Professional Wrestling for Animals

When an **Octopus** wrestles a **BOA CONSTRICTOR**

it's hard to figure out who's winning.

THE LAY-UP

There's a pass across court. Right to me. I'm in the clear. I take off downcourt. Dribbling, running.

A defender blocks me, but I make a little move and get around him. All clear in front of me! Just keep dribbling and don't screw it up.

Now for the lay-up. I've done this a thousand times before. I could make this basket blindfolded. I go up.........

It's out again! .... Noooo! It's almost in. Oh, no! It goes around, around, around. It's on the rim. It's no around, around,

No. No. No. No. No. No. No. No. No. No. No. No. No. No. No. No. No. No. No. No. No. No. No. No. No. No. No. No. No. I was robbed. I *never* miss that shot.

Mom Says, "No New Pets!"

RIP
1998
SSSAMMY
SSSNEAKY SSSNAKE

You never should have crawled into the La-Z-Boy

1999
DIGGY
OVERACTIVE HAMSTER
—
HE BROKE HIS NECK IN THE EXERCISE WHEEL

HERE LIES
PIRATE THE CAT
SHE STOLE HER LAST CHICKEN LEG IN 1997

RIZZO
2002
EXCELLENT RAT
CHEWED TO LIVE, LIVED TO CHEW
—BUT NOT THE TOASTER CORD

2000
DIGGY II
YOUR INSIDES FELL OUT YOUR BUTT
—
GROSS!

KNUCKLEHEAD
2004
A PARAKEET WE ALL LOOKED UP TO
—
WATCH OUT FOR CEILING FANS IN HEAVEN

"Why not?"

"The backyard is full."

BLOODCURDLING SCREAMS

My sister makes this cool noise
when she's in the shower
and I flush the toilet.

AAARRAAAAAAA

HooHooHooHooHoo O o wOwOwHooHooooHoo

OWOMOWOMOwOwHOOHoo

GGHooOWOMOwo

RSRRGG

RSRPGG

HOTHOT HOTHOT YIKES HOTHOTHOT HOTHOTHOT HOTHOTHOTHOTHOTHOTHOT HOTHOT

Wait till I get
my hands
on you, Robert!
You did that
on purpose.

Spew Machine

If I designed a roller coaster, you'd really have reason to spew. Of course, I'd have the usual stuff like loop-de-loops. But I'd make them go much faster. Then I'd have that's when you'd hit the rim of an ice-cave vortex. It's like the inside of a frozen tornado that takes you swirling and around down this slippery drain, around and around until you're so dizzy that you can't even focus. Finally, you'd be in the cannon. BANG! ZOOM! Into the air, where you'd peak and then just free-falling drop, until the p a r a c h u t e opened.

Which it always would.
Well, 90% of the time, anyway.

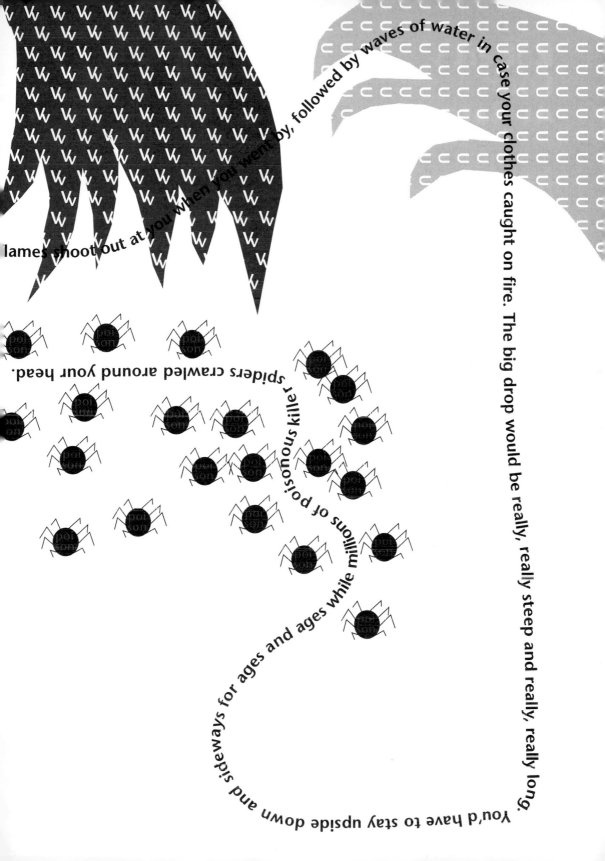

...lames shoot out at you when you went by, followed by waves of water in case your clothes caught on fire. The big drop would be really, really steep and really, really long. You'd have to stay upside down and sideways for ages and ages while millions of poisonous killer spiders crawled around your head.

Robert's Four At-Bats

FIRST INNING: Robert hits a long fly ball to deep, deep, deep center field. It looks tags up and races to third. SAFE!

A wild pitch! Robert breaks for home. It'll be close. He sli-i-i-i-des. SAFE!

THIRD INNING: Robert smashes a line drive, but the shortstop

FIFTH INNING: A bouncing ground ball to the second baseman

BOTTOM OF THE SEVENTH: It's all tied up. Robert comes to bat and

Robert takes off for first. He sees the right fielder boot the ball, so he makes the turn and heads for second. He

out by a step. Shoot!

Cougars win!
Cougars win!
Cougars win!

like it might be out of here! The center fielder goes back, back, back to the fence . . . and makes the catch. Rats!

leaps and makes a fantastic grab. Darn it.

The next batter flies deep to right. Robert

It takes a wicked hop, but he snags it and

lines a solid hit

can't see the ball so he sli-i-i-i-i-des... SAFE!

to right. The outfielder misjudges the bounce and bobbles the ball.

fires it

over to first. It's close, but Robert is

SICK DAY

When you flush a toilet in the Northern Hemisphere, the water drains in a clockwise direction. They say it goes counterclockwise in the Southern Hemisphere. I try to think about how interesting that is while I'm kneeling here, but all I can think about is the disgusting taste in my mouth.

New Game, Old Computer

Neutrina is totally tough,
totally chill,
totally indestructible.
She enters the Black Cave of Subatomica.

She makes a perfect cliff dive

into the toxic
Muon Marsh.

She jumps from
to   rock
rock   to
rock
across the
Lepton Lava Lake.

She leaps to grab a **Pion Vine**
In the
Electro-
Rain
Forest.

She swings
in jerky slo-mo
over the abyss
and just freezes.

The little hourglass

flips and flips and flips and
flips and flips and flips.

The computer crashes.
Neutrina is gone—vaporized
into a billion little atoms
scattered someplace
in the hard drive.

Defeated by a
senile computer and
my totally cheap father.

Robert's
Bed

I like sleeping over. Your room is so cool.

I will. You've got totally superior stuff.

Let's talk for a while.

How come you always win at chess?

I think it's because you're four years older.

I'm going to practice a lot, and
next time we come to visit, I'll beat you.

I like *Huggin' the Rail.* I can win that game.

Don't be a sore loser.

Great! What?

Okay, I'll start. . . .

. . .

. . .

Hey! No fair.

CONVERSATION

Cousin Paul's
Bed

Knock yourself out.

No. I mean it. Knock yourself out—shut up,
be quiet, go to sleep.

You talked all day. You never shut up.
Now go to sleep.

I'm smarter than you.

No, it's because I'm smarter.

I'll still be four years older. And I'll still be smarter.

It's a stupid board game. It's just luck. Whoever
rolls the highest number wins. No skill. All luck.

I have a game we can play.

Who can stay quiet the longest. Ready, set, GO!

. . .

. . .

. . .

Nobody ever actually forbid me to shoot off fireworks. Maybe I should have known better, but *technically* I wasn't disobeying.

It was cool, though.

The rocket went up very nicely, flying in a graceful arc up over the garage, heading toward

I lit the fuse and watched it burn down.

I'd wrapped my sister's math homework around the tube.

the front yard. Then it exploded,

little hunks

of algebra

sparks shooting out

in every direction

blasting apart

going nova

a tiny star

and then

the pieces

fluttering

down

like

a

beautiful

confetti

parade for

Einstein.

I am *so* grounded.
And my parents made me
apologize to my sister.
But it's not *all* bad.
Now she's not talking to me.

Just Mow the Lawn

It doesn't hurt the lawn when you mow it, Robert.
It's just grass.
And that's the lamest excuse you've come up with yet.

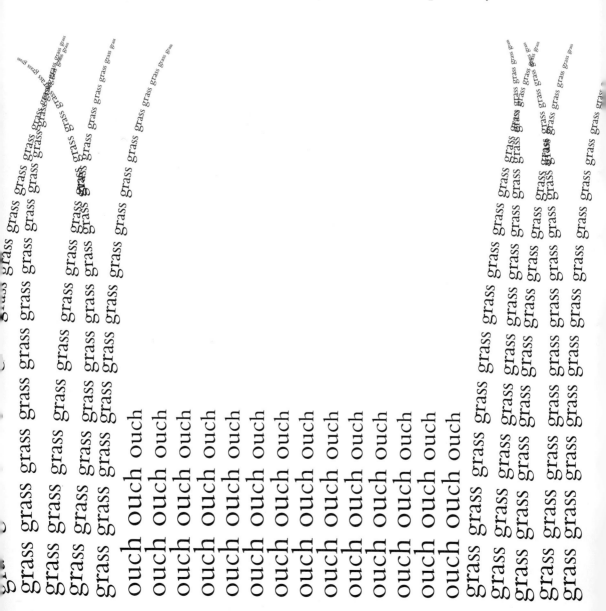

Stop Playing with Your Food!

I ONLY like spaghetti.
It's exactly the same, Robert. Pasta is pasta. By the way, you spelled linguine wrong.
I don't care. It's flat and it's stupid.
Put some tomato sauce on it, you'll never know the difference.
I already know the difference! I'm just going to leave it plain so I can hate it more.

So I've been sitting here for an hour because I have to eat everything on my plate.

THE CAST

I was on my porch
when you came down
the hill. I never
knew a bike could
go that fast.
Tommy Z.

I wish I could see the
inside of an ambulance!
I bet it was great.
Holly S.

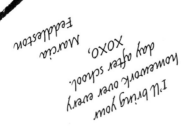

I'll bring your
homework over every
day after school.
XOXO,
Marcia
Feddleston

Nice work, bro!
You'd do anything to get
out of chores.
Sis

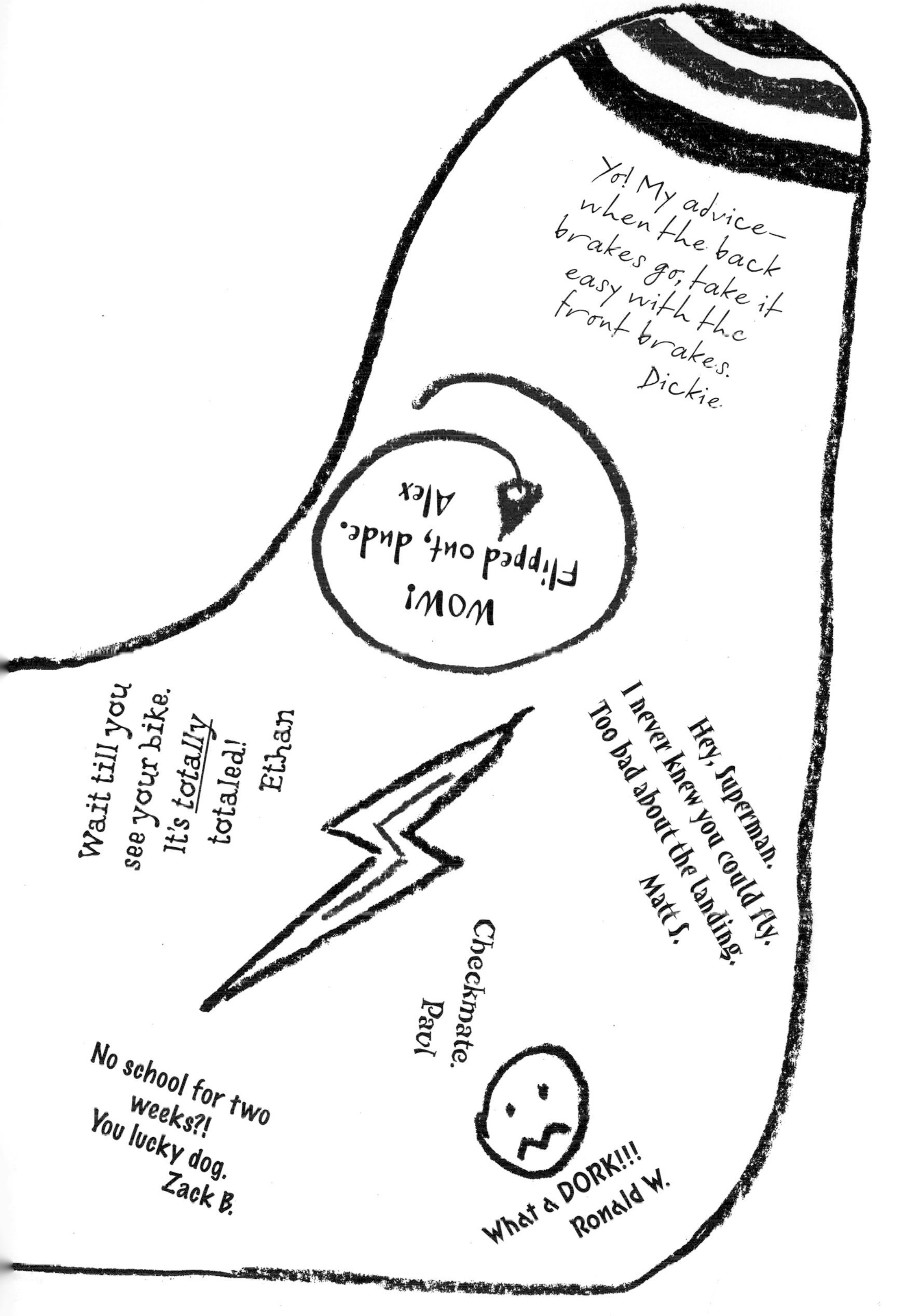
Yo! My advice— when the back brakes go, take it easy with the front brakes. Dickie
WOW! Flipped out, dude. Alex
Wait till you see your bike. It's totally totaled! Ethan
Hey, Superman. I never knew you could fly. Too bad about the landing. Matt S.
Checkmate. Paul
No school for two weeks?! You lucky dog. Zack B.
What a DORK!!! Ronald W.

A Note from the Author

THE
LITTLE
HOUSE

Building
a poem is like
building a little house.
You start
with some bricks—
a pile of   words.
They're
all mixed up.   There is
no order.
They keep tumbling all over each other.

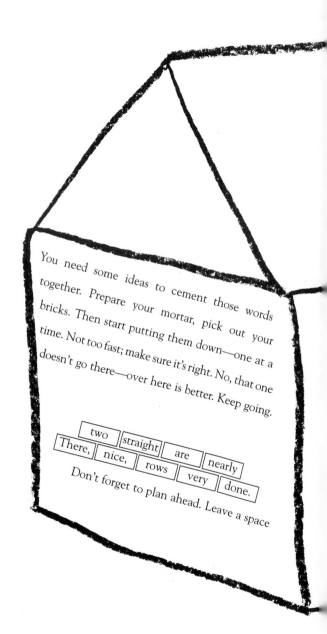

You need some ideas to cement those words together. Prepare your mortar, pick out your bricks. Then start putting them down—one at a time. Not too fast; make sure it's right. No, that one doesn't go there—over here is better. Keep going.

There,	two	straight	are	nearly
	nice,	rows	very	done.

Don't forget to plan ahead. Leave a space

for other people to get

for the door. There has to be a way

in (and for

you to get out). Put in

too: a place to sit in your

a window

sturdy new poem and look

out and see

if the

world looks any different.

These poems were written on a Macintosh G4 using QuarkXPress Software.
The drawings were done with a Bristol China Marker and touched up in Adobe Photoshop.
The poems are set in the following typefaces:

Airstream ITC
Angryhog ITC
Bembo
Caflisch Script
Centaur
CHARLEMAGNE
Clover ITC
Courier New
Django ITC
Fenice ITC
Galliard ITC
Adobe Garamond
Gill Sans Condensed
Goudy Old Style
Grapefruit ITC
Jiggery Pokery ITC
Jott
Kristen Normal ITC
Kumquat ITC
Lingo ITC
Lubalin Graph
Lucida Handwriting
Ludwig ITC
Marker Felt
Medici Script
Sand
Stone Informal
Stone Sans
Tapioca ITC
TRAJAN
Uncle Stinky
&
✳❀□❊ ❖✤■✳❀◉▼▲ (Zapf Dingbats)